DISCARDED

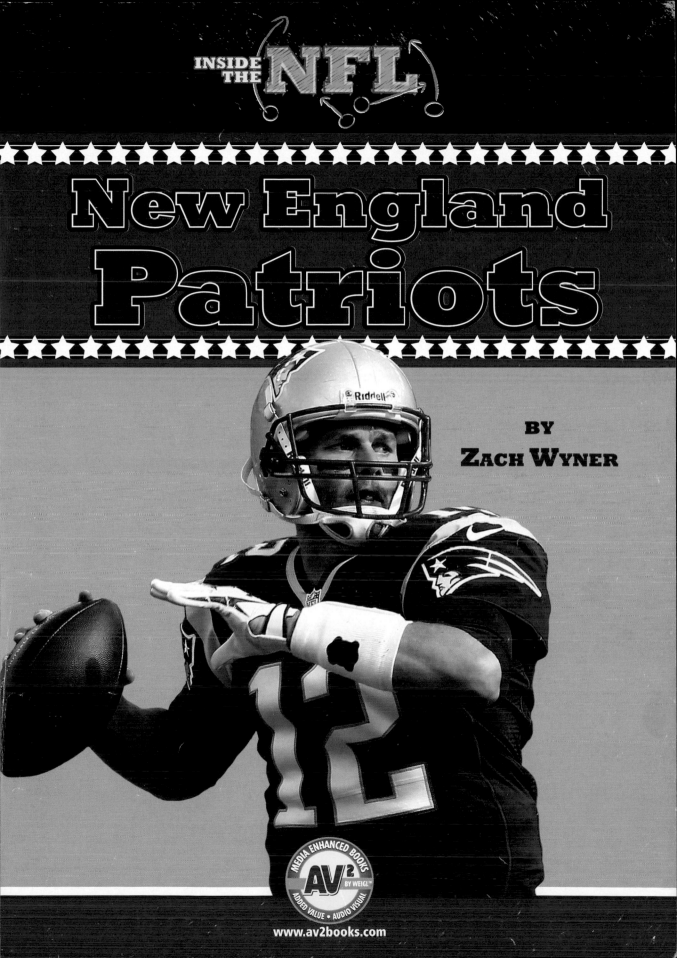

INSIDE THE NFL

New England Patriots

BY
ZACH WYNER

www.av2books.com

AV² provides enriched content that supplements and complements this book. Weigl's AV² books strive to create inspired learning and engage young minds in a total learning experience.

Your AV² Media Enhanced books come alive with...

Audio
Listen to sections of the book read aloud.

Key Words
Study vocabulary, and complete a matching word activity.

Video
Watch informative video clips.

Quizzes
Test your knowledge.

Go to **www.av2books.com**, and enter this book's unique code.

BOOK CODE

U 4 6 7 7 2 9

Embedded Weblinks
Gain additional information for research.

Slide Show
View images and captions, and prepare a presentation.

AV² by Weigl brings you media enhanced books that support active learning.

Try This!
Complete activities and hands-on experiments.

... and much, much more!

Published by AV² by Weigl
350 5ᵗʰ Avenue, 59ᵗʰ Floor
New York, NY 10118
Websites: www.av2books.com   www.weigl.com

Library of Congress Control Number: 2014930828

ISBN 978-1-4896-0854-3 (hardcover)
ISBN 978-1-4896-0856-7 (single-user eBook)
ISBN 978-1-4896-0857-4 (multi-user eBook)

Printed in the United States of America in North Mankato, Minnesota
1 2 3 4 5 6 7 8 9 0 18 17 16 15 14

052015
WEP150314

Project Coordinator Aaron Carr
Art Director Terry Paulhus

Photo Credits
Every reasonable effort has been made to trace ownership and to obtain permission to reprint copyright material. The publishers would be pleased to have any errors or omissions brought to their attention so that they may be corrected in subsequent printings.

Weigl acknowledges Getty Images as its primary image supplier for this title.

New England Patriots

CONTENTS

Introduction

The transformation of the New England Patriots is one of the most dramatic in the history of professional football. This team could not find a permanent home for more than a decade, and they won only a single playoff game in 25 years. The Patriots were also on the losing end of one of the most spectacular blowouts in **Super Bowl** history. After finding their way under new ownership and a new coach, however, the Patriots won 11 division titles in 13 years. They have become of the strongest teams in the National Football League (NFL).

From 2003 to 2012, the Patriots set an NFL record for most wins in a decade, with 126.

Under head coach Bill Belichick, the three-time Super Bowl champion Patriots have been so dominant and feared that they have come to share a nickname previously reserved for Major League Baseball's New York Yankees, "The Evil Empire."

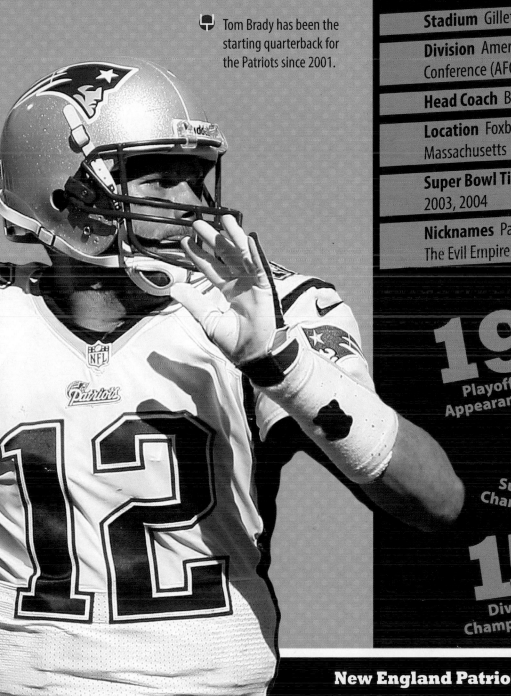

Tom Brady has been the starting quarterback for the Patriots since 2001.

Stadium Gillette Stadium

Division American Football Conference (AFC) East

Head Coach Bill Belichick

Location Foxborough, Massachusetts

Super Bowl Titles 2001, 2003, 2004

Nicknames Pats, The Evil Empire

19
Playoff Appearances

3
Super Bowl Championships

15
Division Championships

History

VICTORY

In 2003 and 2004, the Patriots became the eighth, and most recent, team to win back-to-back Super Bowls.

⨆ When Drew Bledsoe retired in 2007, he was 5th in NFL history in pass attempts and completions, 7th in passing yards, and 13th in touchdown passes.

n 1971, one year after the **American Football League (AFL)**-NFL **merger,** the Boston Patriots moved into Foxboro Stadium and changed their name to the New England Patriots. Despite winning a division title in 1978 and getting great play from future Pro Football **Hall of Famers** Mike Haynes and John Hannah, the Pats were never perceived as Super Bowl contenders.

Ignited by fullback Craig James and wide receiver Irving Fryar, the 1985 Patriots shocked the football world with three straight road playoff wins. In Super Bowl XX, however, they ran into Mike Ditka's Chicago Bears and were crushed, 46-10. Future hall of fame coach Bill Parcells arrived in New England in 1993 and, with the help of quarterback Drew Bledsoe and running back Curtis Martin, the Pats rapidly improved. In 1996, they won their second American Football Conference (AFC) Championship, but lost to the Green Bay Packers in Super Bowl XXXI.

The final stage of the Pats' transformation began when owner Robert Kraft hired coach Bill Belichick in 2000. In Belichick's second season at the helm, an injury to Drew Bledsoe put rookie quarterback Tom Brady on the field. Since that game, Brady and Belichick have won 11 AFC Eastern Division titles, five AFC Championships, and three Super Bowls.

⌐ In the 30 years before Bill Belichick arrived, the Patriots played in two Super Bowls. During the Belichick years, the team has played in five.

The Stadium

Gillette Stadium seats 68,000 cheering fans.

On September 9, 2002, the Super Bowl Champion New England Patriots played their first-ever game at Gillette Stadium, a Monday Night Football game against the Pittsburgh Steelers. The Pats won the game, 30-14, ushering in a new era of Patriots football in style. Located next to the old Foxboro Stadium in Foxborough, Massachusetts, Gillette Stadium is about 21 miles (34 kilometers) from Boston and 20 miles (32 km) from Providence, Rhode Island. The stadium was built at a price tag of $325 million, but it was privately funded. This meant that taxpayers did not have to share the cost of such an expensive construction project.

Since Robert Kraft bought the team in 1994, the Patriots have sold out every home game.

Gillette Stadium's unique design includes a lighthouse at its entrance as well as a bridge, modeled after Longfellow Bridge, which connects Boston's Beacon Hill neighborhood with Cambridge. In 2010, new high-definition scoreboards replaced the old ones, giving Gillette Stadium one of the largest HD scoreboards in professional football. In its brief lifetime, Gillette Stadium has hosted some memorable events, including four AFC Championship games. In the 12 years since moving into Gillette, the Pats have a home playoff win-loss record of 10-3.

Hungry Pats fans head to Smokehouse Grill to feast on flame-broiled half-pound Angus burgers and golden french fries.

Where They Play

CANADA

Washington
30

Oregon

Montana

North Dakota

Minnesota

Lake Superior

Idaho

South Dakota

Wisconsin
23

22

29

Nevada

Wyoming

Iowa

24

15

Utah

Nebraska
14

13

Illinois

California

Colorado

Kansas

Missouri
31

UNITED STATES

16

Arizona

New Mexico

Oklahoma

Arkansas

32

Pacific Ocean

Texas

Mississippi

17

Louisiana

Alaska

Hawai'i

MEXICO

12

27

Gulf of Mexico

0   500 Miles
0   500 km

0   100 Miles
0   100 km

AMERICAN FOOTBALL CONFERENCE

EAST
★ 1 Gillette Stadium
2 MetLife Stadium
3 Ralph Wilson Stadium
4 Sun Life Stadium

NORTH
5 FirstEnergy Stadium
6 Heinz Field
7 M&T Bank Stadium
8 Paul Brown Stadium

SOUTH
9 EverBank Field
10 LP Field
11 Lucas Oil Stadium
12 NRG Stadium

WEST
13 Arrowhead Stadium
14 Sports Authority Field at Mile High
15 O.co Coliseum
16 Qualcomm Stadium

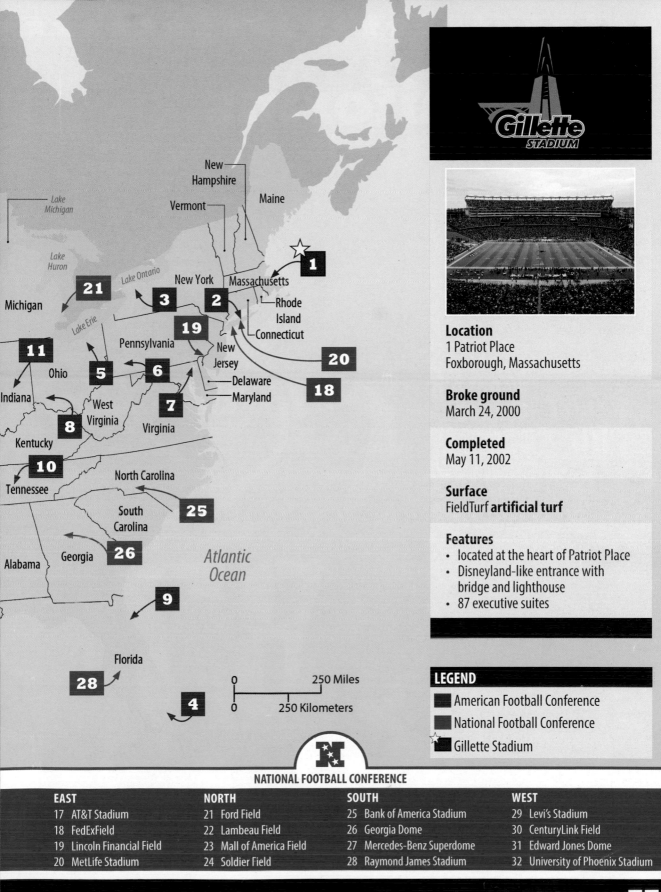

Gillette
STADIUM

Location
1 Patriot Place
Foxborough, Massachusetts

Broke ground
March 24, 2000

Completed
May 11, 2002

Surface
FieldTurf **artificial turf**

Features
· located at the heart of Patriot Place
· Disneyland-like entrance with bridge and lighthouse
· 87 executive suites

LEGEND
▪ American Football Conference
▪ National Football Conference
☆ Gillette Stadium

Lake Michigan
Lake Huron
Lake Ontario
Lake Erie

New Hampshire
Vermont
Maine
Massachusetts
Michigan
New York
Rhode Island
Connecticut
Pennsylvania
New Jersey
Delaware
Maryland
Ohio
Indiana
West Virginia
Virginia
Kentucky
Tennessee
North Carolina
South Carolina
Georgia
Alabama
Florida
Atlantic Ocean

1 **2** **3** **5** **6** **7** **8** **9** **10** **11** **18** **19** **20** **21** **25** **26** **28** **4**

0 — 250 Miles
0 — 250 Kilometers

NATIONAL FOOTBALL CONFERENCE

EAST	NORTH	SOUTH	WEST
17 AT&T Stadium	21 Ford Field	25 Bank of America Stadium	29 Levi's Stadium
18 FedExField	22 Lambeau Field	26 Georgia Dome	30 CenturyLink Field
19 Lincoln Financial Field	23 Mall of America Field	27 Mercedes-Benz Superdome	31 Edward Jones Dome
20 MetLife Stadium	24 Soldier Field	28 Raymond James Stadium	32 University of Phoenix Stadium

The Uniforms

WARDROBE CHANGE

The Patriots have changed uniforms three times, which is more than their Boston neighbors, the Red Sox and Celtics, combined.

In 2011, Rob Gronkowski became the first tight end to lead the league in touchdown receptions.

The Patriots' uniforms have gone through many changes. Jersey colors alternated throughout the years, with the team wearing red at home and white jerseys on the road. They paired red pants with the white jerseys, and paired their white pants with the red jerseys.

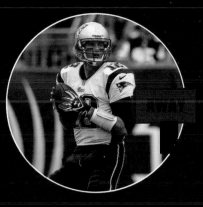

The Pats went through a major makeover in 1993, changing their **logo** and their colors. Home jerseys became blue and road jerseys were all white. In 2000, the Pats added silver to the uniforms. Since then, blue, silver, white, and red are the regularly worn colors.

The Pats' current **alternate uniform**, a red jersey and white pants, is a similar to the uniforms worn in the early years of the franchise.

⊔ NFL uniforms are designed to be lightweight and breathable, so players can make great plays and celebrate with ease.

The Helmets

RED, WHITE, AND BLUE

Pat Patriot was a soldier of the American Revolution and New England's primary logo until 1993.

⅃ The American flag began to appear on the back of all NFL helmets soon after the attacks of September 11, 2001.

In the AFL's **inaugural** season in 1960, the New England Patriots wore white helmets featuring a blue three-cornered hat logo. These helmets were short-lived, as "Pat Patriot" replaced them in 1961. "Pat Patriot" was a man dressed in Revolutionary War clothing with a red three-cornered hat, a blue shirt, white pants, and red socks. Posed in a **three-point stance**, Pat held a football in his right hand as though he was prepared to **hike**, and his face was locked in a sneer.

In 1993, the Patriots changed their uniforms to include the "Flying Elvis" and the logo remains to this day. The "Flying Elvis" was named for its resemblance to the famous rock singer. He wears a blue cap with a white star, and the tail of his cap is red.

NFL players often wear gloves to help them catch the ball, and to protect their hands from injury.

The Coaches

148 Through the 2013 season, Bill Belichick and Tom Brady have combined for the most wins of any player/coach duo in NFL history, with 148.

Bill Belichick is well-known for wearing a hooded sweatshirt, a hoodie, on the sidelines.

Few coaches have been given more credit for transforming a franchise than Bill Belichick. However, before Belichick arrived in New England, a tradition of fine coaching was already in place. Coaches like Raymond Berry and Bill Parcells established a tradition of discipline and creativity in New England.

RAYMOND BERRY

Raymond Berry was a six-time **Pro Bowler** and two-time NFL Champion with the Baltimore Colts. In six seasons at the helm, Berry coached the Pats to five winning seasons and a Super Bowl appearance. His 1985 Patriots were the first NFL team to advance to the Super Bowl by winning three straight games.

BILL PARCELLS

Having twice coached the New York Giants to Super Bowl titles, Pats fans believed that Parcells could turn the team around. In four years, Parcells won two Coach of the Year Awards and coached the Patriots to an AFC Championship.

BILL BELICHICK

Words cannot say what Bill Belichick has meant to the New England Patriots. As the team's head coach and **general manager**, Belichick has had control over all aspects of the Patriots. He has used this control to lead the Patriots to 11 playoff appearances in 14 seasons. With quarterback Tom Brady, Belichick has created a winning tradition.

The Mascot

Though Pat Patriot was replaced as the team's logo, he found work as the team's mascot.

While Pat Patriot is no longer on the Patriots' helmets, fans can still get a glimpse of the revolutionary soldier at every Patriots home game. Voted one of the top 10 mascots in the NFL by *Sports Illustrated Kids*, Pat Patriot ranks right up there with Tom Brady and Bill Belichick as the face of the Patriots' franchise.

⯆ Some members of the End Zone Militia are full-time Revolutionary War re-enactors.

Pat Patriot is the creation of *Boston Globe* artist Phil Bissell, who developed the logo back in 1960 when the Patriots were playing their first AFL season. In their second season, Pat was featured on the Patriots' helmet. He remained there for 35 years. These days, Pat Patriot patrols the sidelines during home games and leads members of the End Zone Militia, who are fans dressed up in Revolutionary War clothes, in a touchdown salute.

⯆ Pat Patriot's uniform is not the same as it was on the team's original helmet. Instead, Pat wears the current Patriots' silver and blue.

Legends of the Past

Many great players have suited up in the Patriots blue and red. A few of them have become icons of the team and the city it represents.

Ty Law

Ty Law was a key member of a Patriots' defense that helped the franchise capture four AFC Championships, and three Super Bowl titles. At 6 feet tall and 200 pounds, he was a big, physical cornerback. Law used his strength to slow down opposing wide receivers while utilizing his speed to make big plays. In his career, Law led the NFL in interceptions twice, made six Pro Bowls, and was named to the NFL 2000s All Decade Team. He was also an important member of the 2003 Patriot defense that recorded 29 interceptions, while only allowing 11 passing touchdowns.

Position Cornerback
Seasons 15 (1995–2009)
Born February 10, 1974, in Aliquippa, Pennsylvania

Drew Bledsoe

Position Quarterback
Seasons 14 (1993–2006)
Born February 14, 1972, in Ellensburg, Washington

On the heels of a season in which they posted a 2-14 record, the Pats selected All American Drew Bledsoe with the first pick in the 1993 **NFL Draft**. At 6 feet, 5 inches tall and 240 pounds, Bledsoe was a big, powerful presence under center. He also had a strong arm. In nine seasons with New England, Bledsoe made four Pro Bowls, set a then-Patriot record for passing yards (29,657), and led the Pats to an AFC Championship in 1996. When Tom Brady went down with an injury in the 2001 AFC Championship Game, Bledsoe came off the bench to beat the Pittsburgh Steelers and set up the Patriots' first Super Bowl win.

Adam Vinatieri

As a member of the New England Patriots from 1996 to 2005, Adam Vinatieri made two Pro Bowls and twice led the league in field goal percentage. However, it was his playoff and Super Bowl heroics that made Vinatieri a sports legend. Vinatieri earned the nickname "Mr. Clutch" during a 2001 divisional playoff game against the Oakland Raiders. In snow and swirling winds, Vinatieri made a 45-yard kick to send the game into overtime and a 25-yarder to win it. He further enhanced his legend by kicking game winners from 48 and 41 yards as time expired to win Super Bowls XXXVI and XXXVIII.

Position Kicker
Seasons 18 (1996–2013)
Born December 28, 1972, in Yankton, South Dakota

Tedy Bruschi

A two-time Pro Bowler, Tedy Bruschi was a team captain and vocal leader of all three New England Patriots Super Bowl-winning teams. His best season may have come in 2004, when he was named Defensive Player of the Week three times, recorded 123 tackles, 3.5 **sacks**, and forced two fumbles. In January of 2005, Bruschi suffered from a mild stroke and announced that he would be taking the year off from football to get well. However, Bruschi made a remarkably quick recovery. He returned to the lineup for the start of the 2005 season and earned the NFL's Comeback Player of the Year award.

Position Linebacker
Seasons 13 (2006–2008)
Born June 9, 1973, in San Francisco, California

Stars of Today

Today's Patriots team is made up of many young, talented players who have proven that they are among the best players in the league.

Tom Brady

Tom Brady is on a short list of the NFL's all-time greatest quarterbacks. In his remarkable 14-year career, he has won three Super Bowl titles, five AFC Championships, was named to eight Pro Bowls, and has put up some eye-popping numbers. He owns virtually every Patriots passing record, including single-season passing yards (5,235) and single-season **passer rating** (117.2). Brady set a then-NFL record in 2007 for single-season passing touchdowns with 50. The 199th pick in the 2000 NFL Draft, Tom Brady is a terrific example of what athletes can achieve through hard work and dedication.

Position Quarterback
Seasons 14 (2000–2013)
Born August 3, 1977, in San Mateo, California

Rob Gronkowski

Tight end Rob Gronkowski, also known as "Gronk," exploded onto the NFL scene as a rookie with 10 receiving touchdowns in 2010. The next season, "Gronk" set single-season records for tight ends in receiving yards (1,327) and receiving touchdowns (17). In 2012 and 2013, serious injuries to Gronkowski's back, forearm, and leg kept him sidelined for important games. Many believe that were he healthy for Super Bowl XLVI against the New York Giants, the Patriots would have celebrated their fourth championship. Going into 2014, Pats fans will keep their fingers crossed, hoping that their two-time Pro Bowler will stay healthy.

Position Tight End
Seasons 4 (2010–2013)
Born May 14, 1989, in Amherst, New York

Jerod Mayo

As the 10th overall draft pick in the 2008 NFL Draft, Jerod Mayo began his professional career with very high expectations. In his first season, his 128 tackles earned him the Associated Press Defensive Rookie of the Year award and fulfilled hopes that he would carry on a legacy of great Pats linebackers like Tedy Bruschi, Ted Johnson, Mike Vrabel, and Willie McGinest. Mayo was named a first team **All-Pro** and made his first Pro Bowl in 2010, a year in which he led the team with 175 tackles. After another Pro Bowl season in 2012, a torn pectoral muscle caused him to miss most of the 2013 season.

Position Linebacker
Seasons 5 (2008–2013)
Born February 23, 1986, in Hampton, Virginia

All-Time Records

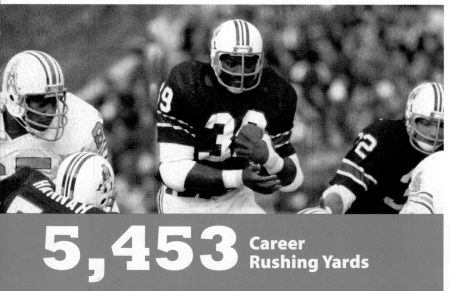

100 Career Sacks

Andre Tippett recorded 100 sacks in 151 career games. His average of 0.66 sacks per game currently ranks as the fourth best in NFL history.

5,453 Career Rushing Yards

Fullback Sam Cunningham was an excellent rusher and receiver, gaining more than 1,000 **yards from scrimmage** four times in his career.

1,635 Single-season Rushing Yards

In 2004, the Patriots signed Pro Bowl running back Corey Dillon. He then set the team record for rushing yards in a season.

49,149

Career Passing Yards

Through 14 seasons, Tom Brady has thrown for 49,149 yards, good for seventh on the NFL's all-time list. He threw for a Patriot-record 5,235 yards in 2011.

23 Single-season Receiving Touchdowns

On the Pats' record-setting offense of 2007, Randy Moss recorded 1,493 receiving yards and caught an NFL-record 23 touchdown passes.

Timeline

Throughout the team's history, the New England Patriots have had many memorable events that have become defining moments for the team and its fans.

1960
In the AFL's inaugural season, the Boston Patriots play home games at Nickerson Field. That stadium is the former home of the National Baseball League's Boston Braves. Despite Butch Songin's 22 touchdown passes, the team struggles, finishing the season 5-9.

1971
One year after the AFL-NFL merger, the Pats move from Boston to Foxborough, Massachusetts and change their name to the New England Patriots. They finish with a losing record for the fifth time in seven years.

In 1985, five Patriots are named to the Pro Bowl.

1960	1965	1970	1975	1980	1985

January, 1986
Under coach Raymond Berry, the Pats win three straight road playoff games to advance to Super Bowl XX. In the franchise's first Super Bowl appearance they lose to Mike Ditka's Chicago Bears, 46-10.

1963
Playing in Fenway Park, home of the Boston Red Sox, future hall of fame linebacker Nick Buoniconti leads the Pats to a division title. The Pats get their first playoff win against the mighty Buffalo Bills, but are blown out in the AFL Championship Game by the San Diego Chargers, 51-10.

1978
Following a terrible injury to wide receiver Darryl Stingley that left him paralyzed from the neck down, the Pats rally to win their first AFC East title. In the first-ever playoff game at Foxboro Stadium, the Pats lose to the Houston Oilers, 31-14.

The Future
With young defensive stars like Jerod Mayo, Chandler Jones, and Dont'a Hightower, the Pats' defense is shaping up to be their best since the mid-2000s. The questions on the mind of every Pats fan are, "Can Rob Gronkowski stay healthy?" and "How long can Brady continue his stellar play?" Grateful fans hope that Brady and Belichick's remarkable run will feature one more title.

1994
St. Louis businessman James Orthwein offers Robert Kraft $75 million to buy out the remainder of the team's lease at Foxboro Stadium, so he could move the Patriots to St. Louis. Kraft rejects the offer and instead buys the Patriots for $175 million, saving football in New England. The Pats respond by making the playoffs for the first time since 1986.

In 2008, the Patriots are the first team ever to go undefeated in a 16-game season, but their hopes of a perfect season are dashed when they suffer a 17-14 loss to the New York Giants in Super Bowl XLII.

1990	1995	2000	2005	2010	2015

In the 2000 NFL Draft, the Patriots select Tom Brady with the 199th pick.

February 2002
In Super Bowl XXXVI, the Patriots face the previous season's Super Bowl champion St. Louis Rams. Two fourth-quarter touchdowns by the Rams tie the game at 17 with 90 seconds remaining. Brady responds, calmly driving the Pats down the field. Adam Vinatieri hits the game-winning 48-yard field goal as time expires.

2013
Despite the departure of Wes Welker to Denver and season-ending injuries to Jerod Mayo, Vince Wilfork, and Rob Gronkowski, the Patriots go 12-4 and win their 11th AFC East title in 13 years.

Write a Biography

Life Story

A person's life story can be the subject of a book. This kind of book is called a biography. Biographies often describe the lives of people who have achieved great success. These people may be alive today, or they may have lived many years ago. Reading a biography can help you learn more about a great person.

Get the Facts

Use this book, and research in the library and on the Internet, to find out more about your favorite Patriot. Learn as much about this player as you can. What position does he play? What are his statistics in important categories? Has he set any records? Also, be sure to write down key events in the person's life. What was his childhood like? What has he accomplished off the field? Is there anything else that makes this person special or unusual?

Use the Concept Web

A concept web is a useful research tool. Read the questions in the concept web on the following page. Answer the questions in your notebook. Your answers will help you write a biography.

Concept Web

Adulthood
- Where does this individual currently reside?
- Does he or she have a family?

Your Opinion
- What did you learn from the books you read in your research?
- Would you suggest these books to others?
- Was anything missing from these books?

Childhood
- Where and when was this person born?
- Describe his or her parents, siblings, and friends.
- Did this person grow up in unusual circumstances?

Accomplishments off the Field
- What is this person's life's work?
- Has he or she received awards or recognition for accomplishments?
- How have this person's accomplishments served others?

Write a Biography

Help and Obstacles
- Did this individual have a positive attitude?
- Did he or she receive help from others?
- Did this person have a mentor?
- Did this person face any hardships?
- If so, how were the hardships overcome?

Accomplishments on the Field
- What records does this person hold?
- What key games and plays have defined his or her career?
- What are his or her stats in categories important to his or her position?

Work and Preparation
- What was this person's education?
- What was his or her work experience?
- How does this person work; what is the process he or she uses?

Trivia Time

Take this quiz to test your knowledge of the New England Patriots.
The answers are printed upside-down under each question.

1 Who is the Patriots' all-time leader in passing yards?

A. Tom Brady

2 Who set the Patriots' single-season rushing record in 2004?

A. Corey Dillon

3 Which Patriots' receiver set an NFL record with 23 touchdown receptions in a single season?

A. Randy Moss

4 Where did the Pats play their home games their year they won their first division title?

A. Fenway Park

5 Which Patriot linebacker returned from a stroke and won the NFL's Comeback Player of the Year award?

A. Tedy Bruschi

6 Who purchased the Patriots and kept them from moving to St. Louis, Missouri?

A. Robert Kraft

7 Which Patriot coach led them to their first Super Bowl in the 1985 season?

A. Raymond Berry

8 How many AFC Championships have the Patriots won in their history?

A. Seven

9 Which high-powered offense did the New England Patriots stifle to win Super Bowl XXXVI?

A. St. Louis Rams

10 What logo is currently on the New England Patriots' helmet?

A. "Flying Elvis"

Key Words

All-Pro: an NFL player judged to be the best in his position for a given season

alternate uniform: a uniform that sports teams may wear in games instead of their home or away uniforms

American Football League (AFL): the American Football League (AFL) was a major American Professional Football league that operated from 1960 until 1969, when it merged with the National Football League (NFL)

artificial turf: any of various synthetic, carpetlike materials made to resemble turf and used as a playing surface for football and baseball fields

general manager: the team executive responsible for acquiring the rights to player personnel, negotiating their contracts, and reassigning or dismissing players no longer desired on the team

hall of famers: a group of persons judged to be outstanding in a particular sport

hike: the backwards pass of the football to start the play

inaugural: marking the beginning of an institution, activity, or period of office

logo: a symbol that stands for a team or organization

merger: a combination of two things, especially companies, into one

NFL Draft: an annual event where the NFL chooses college football players to be new team members

passer rating: a rating given to quarterbacks that tries to measure how well they perform on the field

Pro Bowler: NFL players who take part in the annual all-star game that pits the best players in the National Football Conference against the best players in the American Football Conference

sacks: a sack occurs when the quarterback is tackled behind the line of scrimmage before he can throw a forward pass

Super Bowl: the NFL's annual championship game between the winning team from the NFC and the winning team from the AFC

three-point stance: this stance requires one hand to touch the ground, with the other arm touching the thigh

yards from scrimmage: the total of rushing yards and receiving yards from the yard-line on the field from which the play starts

Index

Log on to www.av2books.com

AV² by Weigl brings you media enhanced books that support active learning. Go to www.av2books.com, and enter the special code found on page 2 of this book. You will gain access to enriched and enhanced content that supplements and complements this book. Content includes video, audio, weblinks, quizzes, a slide show, and activities.

AV² Online Navigation

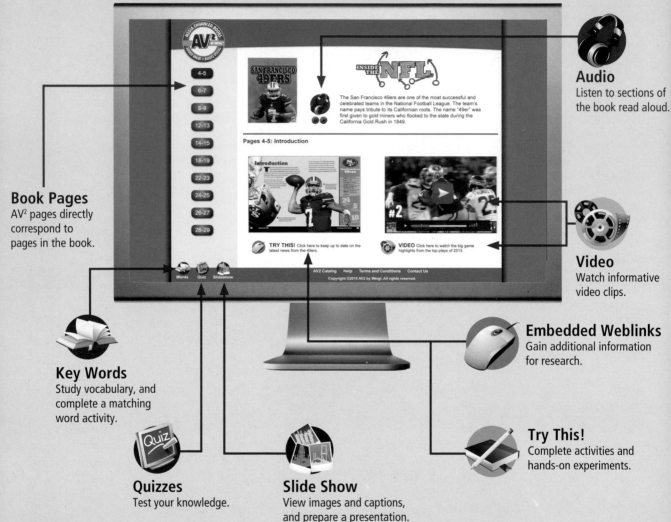

Audio
Listen to sections of the book read aloud.

Book Pages
AV² pages directly correspond to pages in the book.

Video
Watch informative video clips.

Key Words
Study vocabulary, and complete a matching word activity.

Embedded Weblinks
Gain additional information for research.

Quizzes
Test your knowledge.

Slide Show
View images and captions, and prepare a presentation.

Try This!
Complete activities and hands-on experiments.

AV² was built to bridge the gap between print and digital. We encourage you to tell us what you like and what you want to see in the future.

Sign up to be an AV² Ambassador at www.av2books.com/ambassador.